Sifting Through Ashes

Poems by Robert Miller
after photographs and oil paintings by Bruce Gendelman

gefen
publishing house
JERUSALEM ◆ NEW YORK
Est. 1981

Layout and editing by Kate Colangelo
Photographs of oil paintings by Steve Spring

ISBN: 978-965-229-890-4

1 3 5 7 9 8 6 4 2

Gefen Publishing House Ltd.   Gefen Books
6 Hatzvi Street   11 Edison Place
Jerusalem 94386, Israel   Springfield, NJ 07081
972-2-538-0247   516-593-1234
orders@gefenpublishing.com   orders@gefenpublishing.com

www.gefenpublishing.com

Printed in Israel

Contents

Preface

We were raised and educated as Jews, and, of course, we knew a lot about the Holocaust. But in spite of this, we had found it tempting to turn away from the details of this blinding nightmare. We had lived like children watching a horror movie and covering our eyes at the scariest parts. In August 2015, we decided the time for looking away had ended, and we traveled to visit the sites of Holocaust atrocities.

Our prior knowledge of the crimes committed in the name of the Nazi state was grossly inadequate to prepare us for what we experienced. There is power in place. A river will never look the same once you know that not long ago, it had flowed thick with murdered bodies. Pastoral fields lose their serene feel when you realize you are walking atop unmarked graves of innocent victims, buried in indignity, sometimes buried alive.

We spoke to people who were there when the world went mad. Human faces described to us the babies they saw being held by their feet and swung so their heads splattered against trees. They told us, this was to save bullets. They described being forced at gunpoint to strip the dying victims of their clothes before pushing them into ditches, and then pushing more dying naked victims on top of them. We saw the ruins of a mechanized system of extermination that had been built by the people who would be tortured and murdered in the very same structures.

We saw places where courageous, decent people risked their lives to rescue Jews from the tsunami of destruction headed their way. We met people who do not share nationality or religion with the victims, but who strive to keep the memories of the Nazi regime alive as a lesson to all. We saw civilization, returned, like plants and flowers rising from a burned-out forest. We saw the lightness of Krakow, the joy of men and women living their lives in land that had once been fertilized by pure evil. We saw children playing in the town square, oblivious to how darkness can come to a society in the short span of a few years. We met students who had never met a Jew, but who had enrolled in classes to learn about the crimes committed against people whose only offense was their religion or nationality.

We sought to capture some of what we saw and felt in the language of our hearts, words and images to remind ourselves, and anyone who will listen, that it was only yesterday that a civilized society of laws, religious institutions, art and science—a civil nation just like ours—followed a demonic leader into a level of depravity that defies understanding, and yet must be understood.

We have tried to convey the feelings of hope and despair, of altruism and complacency, which we interpret as the Shoah's echoes. We now read, with new eyes, articles about refugees currently fleeing crimes against humanity, people being turned away from safety, because they were born in the wrong place or believe in the wrong God. We now hear, with new ears, the code words used by demagogues to describe the otherness of people who can be used as convenient scapegoats to sacrifice on the altar of nationalism or religious prejudice.

We came away with a deeper understanding of what motivates human behavior when people act individually, and how these motivations can change when they band together to create social contracts. Sometimes groups evolve into a culture of tolerance. Other times, a group's collective motivations mutate into a sinister policy of blame and condemnation of a powerless group of humans.

But, even when it seems we are mere atoms swirling in a chaotic sea, what we do, how we live, does have meaning. The meaning is in the choices we make each day. Auschwitz survivor, Viktor E. Frankl, in his masterpiece, *Man's Search For Meaning*, left us words to live by: "What matters, therefore, is not the meaning of life in general, but, rather, the specific meaning of a person's life at a given moment."

Mountains of Dishware
Auschwitz, Oświęcim, Poland, 2015

Normalcy

Krakow Sunset
Krakow, Poland, 2015

Timeless Sunset

A throaty shout of clouds,
tinged pink gold, this glory,
untainted by dark silver sadness,
a youthful burst of lightness
floating over fairy-tale castles
strutting heavy with history.

We may be at our best, when,
looking up, we see beyond
the reach of mind's shadow,
the sky, keeping its own time,
unburdened by stones, monuments, memory,
its cadence in tune with the present.

The horizon, cleansed and dried,
the sun dropping from sight,
yielding breath after beautiful breath
of normal Krakow life, awaiting the night.
On Earth, it could be yesterday evening,
or nineteen forty-one.

Normal Life
Krakow, Poland, 2015

The Purity of Beginnings

When we speak, but in abstractions, of ephemeral treasures
(love, grace, gratitude, idealism, hope, life),
we may conjure memories of their noble presence,
or of mournful longing when they passed by our grasp,
but we experience and feel nothing of their essence,
no sense of awe and wonder when they reach us
only after being filtered through sterile strips of thought.

Unlike when we are there to see their banners unfurled;
the peace of a child in good dreams' embrace,
a blanket snuggled, keeping colder truths at bay;
the gnarled and spotted hand of an old woman,
as she lifts her evening soup to contented lips;
the calm steely face of a frightened young soldier,
alone at his post and far from his home.

When we are present, we can feel the outer stuff of human reach.
Like now, the trance of these young lovers, lifelong friendship ahead,
the promise of daughters, sons, breakfasts, but, now,
a shared quiet time, after the vows, the communal fest, and, last,
this photo. Kept safe from the camera's vault is a moment,
just after, when bride and groom, with the green day ahead,
know only how good it is to live in this world.

Fragile
Krakow, Poland, 2015

Soap Bubbles, Genocide and Resurrection

A soap bubble is magical to a child:
she can create it herself,
it contains rainbows,
takes dreamy flight,
and can be destroyed without remorse.

A child is magical to her parents:
they create her themselves,
she contains rainbows
in which their dreams take flight;
she can be destroyed without remorse.

We dream of a world of decency,
full of childish pleasures,
imbued with flights of fancy;
a world we can create over the refuse
of the murderers of rainbows.

Horror, Complacency and Denial

From a Child's Eyes
Schindler Factory Museum, Krakow, Poland, 2015

This Is How It Begins

We dig and till at primal footing,
scared, in the thrall of bellowing pigs.
Political blood-colored lipstick
spilling over exceptional fences.
We are the champions. In private,
we welcome the voice that speaks aloud
our shadowed thoughts of rage.
Let us fortify this ground with barbed wire,
the differences gashed in the soil,
keeping the strange strangers away.
Insects do not feel pain, and it is our right,
no, our duty, to destroy the filth and vermin
breeding on our land. What this one did, that one may do.
Better to wipe them all out, crush them into fertile pulp,
enrich our fields with their death.
Give us the sign, lead us to claim what is ours,
what they have taken away.
We have been robbed of our dignity, our humanity;
they must pay for making us wretched.
This is sacred soil and they must be restrained,
perhaps worse, before they gain the strength
to build their own fence.

Artist's Contemplation
Sculptor Richard Edelman in women's barracks, Auschwitz II–Birkenau, Oświęcim, Poland, 2015

The Fools' Fun House

Hate is a mirror
bent by the mind,
obscuring, reflecting
the self we condemn.

We gaze into the eyes
of the other, seeing nothing,
nothing but ourselves.

Our frightened loathing,
what we are not,
yields tumorous growths,
memories of power never held.

Someone is to blame.
You watch the enemy, twisted.
You can have no mercy
for the wretched soul you see.

Barrack Vista
Auschwitz II–Birkenau, women's slave barrack, second tier, Oświęcim, Poland, 2015

Reflection of Rabbi Rosenthal
Auschwitz II–Birkenau, Oświęcim, Poland, 2015

Between
Auschwitz II–Birkenau, Oświęcim, Poland, 2015

Smell

You would no sooner deny the sense of what is present here
than you would the odor of fish rotting in a room,
although nothing is here now of what was, not really.

No shrunken ghosts, no torturers strutting among diseased and decaying bodies;
gone the fear, the hunger, the endless hunger,
the fences electrified while victims sagged with the deadness of despair.

Perhaps the hopelessness still with us, but all else, gone.
Yet, in another sense, all that happened is here, right now,
you cannot ignore this presence, this fog of lingering evil.
A shrine now sterile, yet the past's depravity surrounds you like the air itself.

How can we still perceive in place what is lost forever in time?
The earth, patient, swallows the stench of our worst deeds,
proof that we and it are made of the same stuff,
water and magma, tied to each other as we hurtle through space,
away from, or towards, the pungent past.

Birkenau Barracks Memorial 1
Auschwitz II–Birkenau, Oświęcim, Poland, 2015

Look on My Works, Ye Mighty

Each brick, laid by us to stand and last. We had to kneel to cut them
and stagger to lift them, knowing they would be bent,
with us, our lives' final work, to serve as a monument to depravity.

No one tells us the purpose of our burdens,
but we know. We are slaves to masters
whose single-minded lust for our suffering is unquenchable.

We are peasants, proletarian bankers, quivering fascists, Jews,
appointed enemies of authorities with stern names and angry faces;
shipped as cattle to Birkenau, stripped of clothes, hair, identity, and
committed to the service of their machine.

This machine, a triumphant achievement of scientists, politicians, engineers and soldiers,
its gears churning, working towards our inexorable destruction.
Form complementing function, what malevolent genius
in having the murderers' alibi built
by those to be buried in memory's dungeon!

Yesterday we lift, today we fall, tomorrow all gone.
Only traces escape, like prayer into an impenetrable sky.

Oil Paintings

Birkenau Barracks Memorial 1
2015
Oil painting on canvas
8 x 5 feet

Birkenau Barracks Memorial 2
2015
Oil painting on canvas
8 x 5 feet

Birkenau Barracks Memorial 4
2015
Oil painting on canvas
8 x 5 feet

Ashes

Portal
Auschwitz II–Birkenau, Oświęcim, Poland, 2015

Burning Dark

You cannot look directly.
This place is like the sun,
daring you to see as it taunts,
ducking behind the moon's darkness.

We come to this faded camp where
the eclipse was once complete.
If you gaze too long,
it changes your view, forever.
But how are you to avert your gaze,
as these gaseous ghosts dissolve
over time into further delusion?

We have no choice but to seek
the light of more forgiving stars
whose rays are not obscured
by searing certainty,
grounded for now on trampled earth, with
pastoral fields a cover-up for the defiled dead.
How can so much seem forgotten?
So much kindling, personal truths,
fists like trees rising up against popular winds,
defending threats perceived or claimed;
flames of conviction consuming soul.

This is the fragile altar around which, in rage,
we pile the tinder of our complacent hopes;
the bedrock on which never again
becomes why not.

Father Patrick Desbois
Tuchów, Poland, 2015

Father Patrick Desbois

We follow this Father
on a tour. He is not a tour guide;
this is not sightseeing.

He cautions us to not ask useless things
of the witnesses we would meet,
like, "How did it feel?"

An old man told Father, and us, his truth,
and showed where the Jews
were stripped, shot, pushed into ditches.

We were the first people this villager
took here. No longer a crime scene—
no trace of proof but the memory of this man.

This old man was here as witness
at the call of Father Patrick,
and was glad to share his story.

Father Patrick, a man of Christ, a wanderer,
devoted to the search for unremembered souls,
lost ancestors not of his tribe.

A good, quiet hero,
he enters churches, preaching
his simple gospel of remembrance.

He asks who remembers. Congregants, elders only,
some will come to him, and show—
farms near towns, the grass hides the bodies.

We did not ask Father why he seeks to hallow
buried ditches before which naked families
waited in the cold to be shot. Useless question.

But here's the thing. He guided us to see—
cursed though we may be with human evil's shadow—
an angel, rising, shedding light; thank you, Father.

Now ... A Great Man
Tuchów, Poland, 2015

Witness

Let me tell you what I saw; I need to tell you what I saw.

Innocent men and women shot and pushed into ditches. Babies smashed against trees.

At gunpoint I stripped the bodies, already dead like their murderers, dead inside first, dead for all to see
who looked, but I am still alive to tell.

Whether or not I want to remember, I do and I must tell.

What is left for an old man to do but tell.

Here is where it happened.

I was not a hero, I was not a collaborator; we were all victims, even the heroes, even the collaborators,
even the perpetrators.

All of us victims of our humanity. The good, the bad, the unthinkable, all by and to humans.

Here is where it happened; please listen to me without judging: You were not there.

No one can understand who was not there. I was there.

I understand enough to know that no one can understand.

But do not think that because it is incomprehensible it did not happen.

It happened and I was there, and I was told by scum with guns to take the clothes off the dead
and almost dead. And cover the dead and dying with more dead and dying,

then with dirt, which moved, and more dirt, then silence, and I was never the same.

I remember some things well. This day, and others like it.

A happy poem about nature I had memorized when I was eight.

Please forgive yourself for being no better than me.

Garden Plot
A resident's flower garden, adjacent to an unmarked massacre site, Tuchów, Poland, 2015

Monuments

Sometimes thoughts break through our pleasant fog
of the one stone we will someday leave behind
to proclaim, "I was here!"
Such a humble desire, in human scale
this want for a stone, an imagined permanence
no less laughable than our grasping for our own.
But it is our right to claim a spot, a plot, an urn.

If humble is our lot, we should then be allotted
a rock of some sort in our name. Not all of us are.
Vast swaths of turf barren of landmarks, fields, marshes,
buildings and streets, above graves with no homage,
lives sucked dry of edifice.
Buried treasure without a map, rare stories
written on the cinders of burnt albums.

We stand near ground newly revealed.
Revealing nothing. We feel the grand emptiness
of bodies which belonged to names,
faces, loved ones, worries and plans.

No rocks left behind; their murders
await the mourning of unexpected strangers.
Birds overhead. A cloudy sky. Silence as witness.

Consecration
Tuchów, Poland, 2015

Weeds

So undemanding for love,

they spring from disregarded ground

shouting one prayer: Life is good!

Heedless of the listening,

it is all in the singing

the praises of earth.

Flowers from dirt,

dirt formed of flowers,

gardens bursting over graves

yielding wild tales of forever.

The Denier
Tuchów, Poland, 2015

Denier

For eons this river has flowed,
picking up detritus of time's erosion, the life on its banks.
More than once it churned with the current of murdered bodies.

Imagine yourself today standing by as it passes.
Imagine a spot hundreds of miles away
where a young lad is skipping stones
across a section where the river moves slow,
the water clearer as it stills.

Imagine the ripples made as the stones skip across.
Imagine waiting for the ripples to make their way
to the distant spot where you stand.

This is memory: ripples across the surface of changing currents and streams,
churning sediment, diluting substance, losing touch with its source.

Imagine now an old man who lived near this river long ago,
when its turbulence had risen far beyond its banks.
He lived in a town with forgotten neighbors,
folks who were carefully tortured or, if lucky, quickly killed.

He speaks up now but did not speak up then.
He tells you the river was always the same.
He tells you he remembers nothing of the atrocities
by the park where he used to picnic,
in the town where he lived and worked,
where the river flowed past his backyard.

He was but one man, and this was long ago.
Yes, terrible things happened, but they happened in secret, he says.
He does not believe he is lying; his thinking depends on the lie.
His memories cannot be brought back to the clearer streams from which they were once cut.
Like the dead bodies moving down-current long ago,
these departed souls, what happened, are in his mind,
rotten, repulsive, removed from the span of human story; gone.

The Dom Katolicki
During the first Aktion, Jews were taken to the Catholic Community Center,
tortured, then marched into the forest, Bolekhiv, Ukraine, 2015

At the DKA

I cannot see what is happening. The soldiers are screaming again;
German voices, Ukrainian voices, the sound of angry laughter.
We have been here so long, one or two days, maybe more.
This room was built to bring a community together,
but not this way, not us against them.

The smell of bodily waste, blood, fear, overpowering;
I am lying face down, my head between my crossed arms,
trying not to move, trying not to breathe too loud,
trying not to shiver from fright, hunger and cold.
I know some of these nasty voices;
people who must have hated us all along.

I know the victims, too.
I hear the cries of our rabbi; they are yelling at him,
making him sing and dance. It is a happy song,
and he is howling in agony as he tries to comply.
I look up ever so slightly, keeping my head down.
I see a man who lives three doors down from us
gleefully torturing the rabbi.

I put my head back down. All is lost. I do not care to live anymore.
I wait my turn to die a horrible death. It will come soon.
I wonder what I could have done differently.
I am a good girl, only fourteen years old:
What did I do to make them hate me so?

The Dom Katolicki Today
Bolekhiv, Ukraine, 2015

Taniawa Forest Massacre Site
950 buried—including the photographer's ancestors, Bolekhiv, Ukraine, 2015

They Still Hate Us
Graffiti over brick facade of the former Jewish department store, Lviv, Ukraine, 2015

Signs

The cities are bright with hope and desire,
The villages calm daily toil,
The smoke does not rise from bodies on fire,
The hatred no longer full boil.

The past is enshrined, on full display
Teaching of prologues to come.
The everyday rhythms allowed to proceed,
The dark truth shares the same sun.

In many nice homes, the stories are told
Of days we would like to forget.
In other nice homes, the old lies still sold
Without a trace of regret.

Walk around, see the walls fresh-defaced,
Swastikas here, stars struck through there,
Outward signs of darkness's escape,
The whispered lies we all share.

We see what we want, we gaze where we choose,
We believe what we want to believe,
We read different stories from the same news,
It's the personal losses we grieve.

The signs of the times are always about,
The graffiti shows who we debase,
More immutable than the self-praises we shout,
They are stamped on our memories' face.

Acceptance, Homage and Hope

Family Tree
Bolekhiv, Ukraine, 2015

Traces of Our Souls

Family, this connector that transcends desire,
the path from which we search, always looking back,
for some map to bring us forward towards contented destiny,
as thinly marked as the memory of a dream;
we are in this way connected always,
entwined in this veil from which we emerged,
the force through which life swims
among misaligned magnets, repelling and attracting,
the magic and embittered moments
weaving their silky shiny sticky web,
glowing with love's vital juice or dying into dust.
We are left with this fabric ripped ragged from our bones
(they even hated our bones),
this skin that remains
even when it does not grow back.

Josef Ber Bruckenstein, Son of Israel Iser
The grave site of the photographer's Great Great Grandfather; Bolekhiv, Ukraine, 2015;
See Nina Edelman's blog: *www.ninaedelman.blogspot.com*

The Last Jew of Lviv
Placing tefillin at dusk, in the ruins of the Great Shul of Lviv, Lviv, Ukraine, 2015

The Last Jew of Lviv

He walks a path well-worn,
the markers laid down by those
who trod before him, through the desert,
following boundaries of law, tradition
and reverence, in search of meaning.

He pays homage to his forbearers
by small daily acts that weave
into the patterns of his life.
Ask him why he lives this way
and he shrugs; the question suggests
there is another way, and to him,
the way he lives is his home.
Not a city, not a town, not a building,
but the sanctuary in his soul where
tradition is the strongest refuge.

There is no one left but him;
the world whizzes past
as he stands firm, holding his ground,
not alone, relishing what once was,
praying for a better tomorrow,
amid a congregation of ghosts.

Lock in the Women
Auschwitz II–Birkenau barracks, Oświęcim, Poland, 2015

Dream Progeny

When we were children, we had no idea
the dreams we had asleep would later become, waking,
the dreams of different children,
the children we would have.

But in those waking dreams, we dreamed less
of the children that would be, than of the children we once were.
Shared dreams, passed over generations, completely intact,
but unremembered, the visions faded in wakefulness.

We breed only hope as we conceive, eagerly and expectantly,
children of the dreams of Abraham, Jesus, Mohammed, Gandhi,
Hitler, Bin-Laden, and the rest.
Dreams are only real when the dreamer believes them.

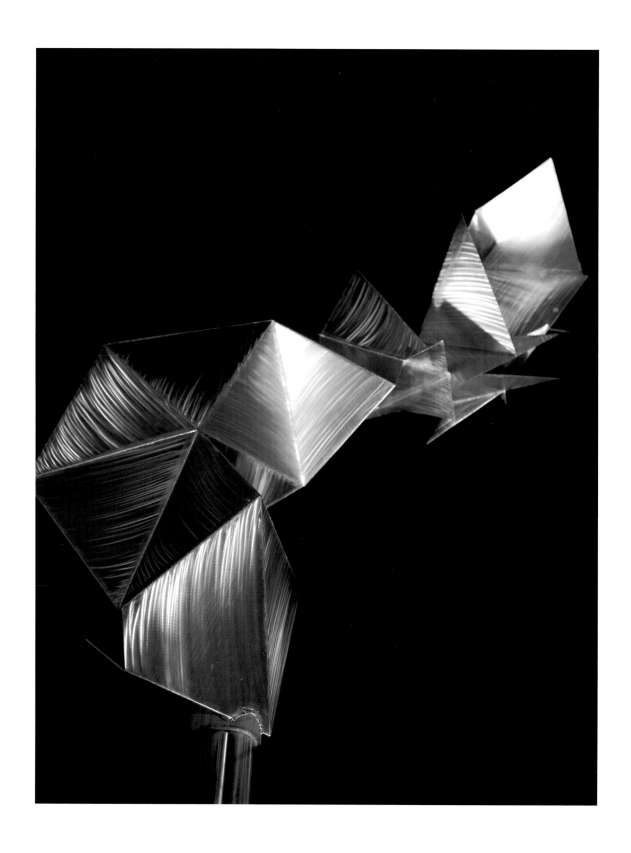

We Have Survived; We Have Created to Remember
Call to Return, a sculpture by Richard Edelman, dedicated at the Krakow JCC, Krakow, Poland, 2015

Shofar Krakow

Sixty-six or so kilometers to the east,
near enough, not long ago,
the darkest depths,
humanity's pit
where no light shined,
when light was prayer.
This is the same world.

We come here to pierce
through consecrated shadows.
Rising above echoes of ashes
reverberate unheard screams.
We stand in awesome
agonized pools of silence
beneath the broken stars.

When pain is so numbing,
too cold to let in,
what is left to do
but sing, dance, love?

Our hearts attuned, let us behold
music of melted metal
forged by Jewish hands,
signifying survival,
this horn, rammed upward
like a gigantic middle finger.

Our song, defiant,
scorning the darkness,
the call of the Shofar
laughing evil into dust.

Afterword

Our visit to the sites of Nazi atrocities took place a mere seven decades after the liberation of the remaining survivors. The criminals had destroyed much of the evidence of their crimes, but, because of magnitude of their destruction, and the careful records they kept, a detailed accounting may be had of the cool, calculated, and methodical annihilation of their Jewish victims. The evidence may be found in the remains of camps, repurposed buildings, farmland, and, of course, in the recounting of the atrocities by living survivors.

This last feature, the eyewitness accounts of living survivors, is a precious thing, as there are very few survivors left. It is we, their heirs, who must continue to keep this history alive.

It is human nature to look back at this savagery with condemnation and say, "never again." But it is also human nature to become complacent, to feel protected in our insulated bubble of modern civilization. We live in the United States, an imperfect place, but one that is founded on law, scientific and engineering achievement, religious tolerance, respect for the arts, and, on the average, a very high standard of living.

So, for the most part, was the German state that elected Adolf Hitler. And there were many decent people living there, some of whom spoke out once Hitler began his program of discrimination, as the precursor to the annihilation of the Jews. But most did not.

While we were in Europe working on this book, politicians throughout Europe and in the United States were reacting to a refugee crisis by fomenting hatred and distrust of people whose only sin was fleeing for their lives. We read the news of these reactions realizing that, while they were based in part on legitimate fear, they were in large part also based on the demagoguery of leaders willing to manipulate fear to further political, social, economic, or religious agendas.

In a world filled with terrorism, fear is a natural and appropriate reaction. We are genetically programmed to protect ourselves. We are also social creatures, and we aggregate in tribal groups, based upon family, nationality, religion, and economic interests. It is part of the human condition to prize individual liberties while being willing to sacrifice them for the greater good of the tribe. When there is a balance between these competing interests, there is peace.

When people are scared enough, however, there is no balance; the reaction is to throw out notions of the importance of the individual, and become warriors in the focused pursuit of vanquishing "others."

It is not "fear itself" we should fear. Our biggest enemy is not fear, not others, not even us as individuals. Our enemy is our human proclivity to become out of balance; to do as a group what we would be unwilling to do as individuals.

The madness of the mob happens when decent voices do not speak out, and mob rule can take place at a national, even an international level. Genocide is the result. Come see what it looks like. Be careful. Don't look away. Speak out.